The Road to Publishing

By Dawn Brotherton

 Blue Dragon Publishing

Published by Blue Dragon Publishing, LLC

PO Box 247

Lightfoot, VA 23090

www.blue-dragon-publishing.com

Copyright © 2018 by Dawn Brotherton

ISBN 978-1-939696-44-1 (paperback)

ISBN 978-1-939696-45-8 (ebook)

Library of Congress Control Number: 2018908586

Printed in the USA

Table of Contents

Introduction 7

Chapter 1: Why Publish?....................... 11

    Define Success 13

    Goals 15

Chapter 2: Your Audience 18

    Target Audience 19

    Who Is Your Competition?...............................22

Chapter 3: What Does It Take?.............. 24

    Practice 25

    Setting Up a Business......................................27

    Writing Time 30

    Building Your Platform Now 32

Chapter 4: Don't Rush to Publish 39

Chapter 5: Editing 45

    Types of Editors...46

    Hiring an Editor 50

    When the Edits Come Back..............................55

Chapter 6: Publishing Options............... 57

    Vanity Press..58

    Traditional Publishing 59

    Self-Publishing...63

    Indie Publishing...67

Chapter 7: Query Letters 72

Research 73

Basic Requirements...............................75

Chapter 8: Agents.................................... 78

Where to Find an Agent 79

Chapter 9: Publicity vs. Marketing 84

Marketing..84

Publicity...88

Selling Yourself...92

Elevator Speech..94

Chapter 10: Selling Your Story 98

Brick-n-Mortar...98

Amazon 101

eBooks...102

Face-to-Face 105

Chapter 11: Self-Publishing Route 107

Font and size 109

Headings, Chapter Spacing............................111

Margins...112

Trim Size 114

ISBN 116

Covers..117

Copyright Page 122

Copyright (www.copyright.gov)......................125

Chapter 12: Printers 128

Traditional Print Run.......................................128

Print-on-Demand 130

Paper Quality 132

Chapter 13: Warehouse/Fulfillment vs Distributor.. 135

Chapter 14: Indie Publishing Route...... 139

Author Input...139

Printing with an Indie.....................................142

Final Thoughts 146

Recommended References:................. 147

Books...147

Websites 147

About the Author 148

Books by Dawn Brotherton................... 150

Introduction

There is so much more to writing than writing. It never ceases to amaze me how much time I spend on my writing career that doesn't involve getting my story on paper.

There is setting up book signings, then creating the signs for it, then the pre-advertising, and, and, and...

Oh, but before you get to that, you need a website, and a Facebook account, Pinterest, Twitter or Snapchat. You need a following. But how do you build a following? A blog? Add it to the list.

How do you learn about what needs to be done? Research the internet, read books in your genre, read books about writing, read books about publishing, join writers' circles, book clubs, and author associations.

Where does marketing come in? Before you're done writing or after? Or somewhere in between? What do you know about marketing? Better read more books, do more research. Maybe attend a seminar or class.

In the meantime, you need to get your cover designed, manuscript edited (multiple times) and storyline boosted. Who needs to sleep? You need to get writing!

It's a long, twisting road to publishing—don't let anyone tell you differently. There's no one path, and results are as varied as the methods to get there.

My journey started as a simple quest to get my story on paper. When I was a second lieutenant in the Air Force, stationed in Missouri as a missile launch officer, I had a stalker. I would delight at the reactions of my audience as I regaled them with the tale of the creepy things that can happen to a young female, working in a man's career field, living alone, rebuilding a 100-year old house single-handedly. After the expected ohs and ahs, my listeners would insist I write it down, some going as far as to assert there should be a movie deal on the table.

As frightening as it was at the time, my experiences don't live up to Hollywood expectations, and I realized this. To satisfy my friends and colleagues, I put pen to paper—or hands to keyboard, as it were—setting a self-imposed deadline at the end of 2010.

Reading through the pages, where the real ending was nothing more than a permanent change of duty assignment, I recognized my life wasn't exciting enough to share with the masses. But, after adding a few murders, the storyline took on a life of its own.

Having never done this before, I reached the end of my draft manuscript and had no one to ask, "now what?" Keep in mind this was 2010, and the resources for self-publishing weren't quite as prolific as they are now.

One of my traits, sometimes positive and sometimes negative, is I have little patience. I want to get things done and move on. The book was written, so I wanted to move on to the next stage—figuring out how to get it published. Where to start? There are plenty of books, blogs, and websites that will feed you bits and pieces, but as I alluded to at the beginning, there is no ONE way to get there.

Let's walk this path together.

I will start by saying, I am not a lawyer and cannot give legal advice. I am also not a tax accountant, so my biggest piece of advice is to find a good one of each.

I am a person who has written and published numerous titles. I have also published works by other authors and helped them realize their dreams. I speak at conferences, teach classes on publishing and work with schools and Girl Scouts to encourage young writers.

Now I'd like to extend my reach and help you. I would never claim to know everything about publishing. It's growing and changing at such a rapid pace, I don't think anyone could ever make that claim. Before you make a decision affecting your life, you owe it to yourself to do some homework.

Chapter 1: Why Publish?

You are a writer. Whether you publish or not, if you are creating a written story or poem, you are a writer.

Why do you want to publish?

You may think this is an easy question, but there's a lot more to it.

Do you want to be a famous writer? Even that's a loaded question. What will make you famous? Selling 100,000 copies? Making lots of money? Having your name on a book jacket? Seeing your book on a shelf in a bookstore?

Maybe your idea is just so good you want to share, or a story has been rattling around in your head for so long you need to get it on paper. Do you have an interesting family history you want to pass on to your kids and many future generations? So then it isn't about the money.

Some writers want to demonstrate themselves as an expert in a particular field. Do you own a business where a book will help your credibility and reach? Perhaps you want a leave-behind for your presentations and talks.

If you are a marketer, you may publish a book to teach others how to apply your suggestions when it comes to advertising. If you are a college professor, the students need a textbook. Why not one you wrote?

Do you like getting free stuff? Most people do. If you have a business with a website, what about giving away a book in exchange for gaining a customer's email address? Think of the book as an advertisement for your business overall.

Name recognition is important. Even if you give away your book for free, your name is getting out there. All advertising is good advertising, right? And if you give away an eBook, no tree was sacrificed for your cause.

Or do you write for the love of writing? That's a great reason as well. If you have a story or information to share, what is more important—money or the exposure? Either answer is acceptable. Your reason is what's important.

Get a notebook.

Why do you want to publish?

Write down your reason. We will refer back to them. It may be a combination of things.

Love of writing
Established Expert
Advertising
Name Recognition
Fame
Textbook
Legacy

Define Success

Now you have established why you want to publish. How will you know when you are successful? The answer is as different as your reason to publish.

What do you consider success? A best-selling author can be defined in many ways. Giving your book away for free may earn you many clicks and put you on your way toward the best-selling ladder, without pocketing a dime.

Highest earning author is different. It is calculated on algorithms taken from sales in certain markets, but not all. So is it really a true representation of highest sales?

If earning a large paycheck is your goal, you have to ask yourself how much work you are willing to endure. If you are willing to put forth the effort, self-publishing can turn you a nice profit. You get to keep most the earnings without the middlemen taking their cut. But it is a lot of work and a lot of mistakes can be made in the process.

If having your book in the window of a large bookstore is your idea of success, that is a different path. You probably want to get an agent and aim for traditional publishing. Those publishers have connections and a marketing reach hard to match.

Pull out your notebook.

What does it mean to you to be an Author?

How do you define success?

Why is writing important to you?

What are your fears about publishing?

Goals

To determine when you are successful—by your own definition—you need to set goals that are measurable.

You need to be realistic when setting your goals. The Huffington Post gives a stark outline of the many now-famous authors and their rejections before fame. This includes Stephen King's first big novel, Carrie, which was rejected 30 times. Janet Evanovich wrote for 10 years before getting published. There is hope for the persistent.

Publisher's Weekly says the average book sells less than 500 copies. Because the big-name authors sell millions, it really skews the score for the rest of us. But that's okay. Go back to why you wanted to write in the first place.

Not everyone can sell millions, or even thousands, but you can sell enough to break even. That was my goal on my first book. After I reached my break-even number (which wasn't very high), I stopped counting how many I sold and started focusing on my next book, and the next.

If you are creating something for your family, organization, or just to see your name in print, there's no need to invest a lot of money on marketing and publicity. But there's no reason not to build a product you can be proud of. And why not take advantage of some of the free resources available to you? You may even earn a little something to offset the money you've paid. With electronic books and print-on-demand, what you put down on "paper" might be out there a long time. Make it worth it.

If you are an expert in something and want to share knowledge through the written word, a book—even a short one—is a great way to lend credibility to your craft. In that case, it's even more important you have a professional looking product, because its quality will reflect your main business venture.

I highly recommend working with someone who can provide you with the service you need. Don't pay money to simply have your book printed. There are many steps before then we'll discuss in this book.

As we travel this road, you will have the opportunity to tweak your goals based on the lessons you learn in this book.

Pull out your notebook.

What is your long-term goal?

Do you have a sales goal? To reach a certain number?

What is your timeline goal?

How much have you set aside to invest?

How much time are you going to invest in selling your book?

Chapter 2: Your Audience

Okay, you now have goals to help make you successful on your own road to publishing. As we move on to the next phase of determining who your target audience is, refer back to why you want to publish to begin with.

If you are writing a family history to pass on to your grandchildren, they and future generations are your target audience.

As leave-behind material, your target audience will probably be the same as your primary business.

It's important to identify your audience when it comes to marketing, and in some cases, even in the writing. You want to use the terminology your reader will understand and relate to.

Target Audience

No one can please everyone. So don't try. Think hard about who you are writing for and who you are trying to reach. The audience will be different for a college textbook than they will be for a romance novel. There may be overlap, but you are targeting the buyer in the moment.

Many people think trade fiction is for everyone. Not true. There are many genres of fiction and just because you like mysteries does not mean you will like a thriller. As you are trying to narrow your target audience, you may feel you are delving into the world of stereotypes. You probably are to some degree, but that's how marketing works. There will always be an exception or outlier, but aiming for center-mass, you will have the best chance of hitting your mark.

Depending on what you're writing, you can be more specific. My middle grade Lady Tigers' series is about a girls' fastpitch softball team. There is no reason a boy can't read the series. Realistically, the books are about a girls' team, therefore my target audience is girls. More specifically, girls who like sports are more likely to read the books, although they don't have to play softball. So I'm trying to sell to parents who want to buy books for their third or fourth grade girls who are sports-minded and like to read.

The more specific you can get when picturing your audience, the easier it will be when determining which marketing strategies to use. We'll talk more about marketing in later chapters.

Pull out your notebook.

Who is your audience?

Who are you writing this book for? Be specific.

o Male or female?

o Age range?

o Education level?Occupation?

o Religious preference?

o Do they live in a specific region
   of the world or a country?

- Democrat, Republican, Independent? Do they even care about politics?

- Gay or straight?

- Married, single or divorced?

- What's the family's living arrangement? Are they boomerang parents whose twenty-something kids live at home? Or is the target market the kids who moved back? Do your readers live in retirement communities?

- Are they part of the sandwich generation, caring for still-at-home kids and elderly parents?

- What are their hobbies and interests?

- Do they travel? If so, where?

- Do they invest money? Or are they in deep debt?

- What business problems keep them up at 3 a.m.?

- What lifestyle problems cause sleepless nights?

- What are their favorite TV programs?

- What magazines might you find on their night stands?

- Do they listen to the radio? Talk radio? Jazz? Hip-hop? NPR?

- What social issues and causes do they care about? Are they activists?

- What influencers (celebrities, experts, thought leaders, famous authors) do they follow?

Who Is Your Competition?

You may think your book is a one-of-a-kind and nothing else is remotely close. With billions of books written and on the market, chances are you have competition. If nothing like it has ever been done, maybe there's a reason. Maybe it doesn't sell or there isn't a following for it. The way you spin your story should be unique, but the basic storyline has probably already been written.

With that in mind, seek out your competition. If you are writing romance, read a few. Take note of what you like or don't like about them. If you find writers you like, follow them on social media; check out their website.

Pull out your notebook.

What authors write the same genre you are writing? Follow them on social media.

Which reviewers gave them reviews? Research how to get your book into reviewer's hands.

Are there any special interest groups for your genre? Check out Facebook and LinkedIn.

Chapter 3: What Does It Take?

Okay, let's work off the premise you want to be published. There are many ways to get there, including self-publishing.

How much time and energy do you want to put into this process? If you are a go-getter and do-it-yourselfer, self-publishing might be right up your alley. But if you have other areas of interest where you want to spend your time, you may prefer to work with an independent publisher or publishing service.

If you aren't in a rush to get the book to market, maybe you should try traditional publishing. You can always fall back to hybrid or self-publishing if you aren't picked up by an agent.

There is still a lot of work involved with traditional publishing. The writer is required to do marketing, participate in publicity and sell themselves through social media or other avenues. And just to get to an agent, you probably have already had your work edited at least once by a reputable editor.

Pull out your notebook.

List your top 3 strengths.

List your top 3 weaknesses.

How much time will you write every week?

How much time a week are you willing to work on the business of publishing?

Practice

I heard a great analogy for this situation. No basketball player plays in an NBA game the first time he picks up the ball. Why do all writers expect their first book to be published? It takes years of practice to sharpen your basketball skills. It will take years of practice to hone your writing skills.

There are many games through high school, and perhaps college, before a player is ready to try out for the big leagues. Be patient with yourself and your writing.

Learn something from every piece you create and improve upon it with every new work of art you generate.

Try different styles, techniques and voices.

And READ! A good writer must also be a reader. I'm sure you have heard this before. The reason you hear it so often is because it's true. Reading for an author is like studying playbooks for an athlete. See how others do it. Note what you like and don't like. Think of ways to do it better.

Writing requires commitment, and publishing requires patience. Having a vision and a plan have proven to be useful in achieving one's goals.

Pull out your notebook.

How many books a year will you read?

What types of books? Same genre you are writing?

Business?

Setting Up a Business

Reading and practicing your craft will improve your writing. Publishing is also a business. You should add a few books about good accounting, legal and marketing practices to your reading list. I will recommend a few throughout this book.

If you are trying to earn money as a writer, you are an entrepreneur. Not all entrepreneurs make money, especially in the first few years. But there are a few things you need to do to set up your writing business.

Before you decide to publish, you need to ensure you have the capital to invest upfront. Every money-making venture is a risk. Writing is no different. Track your expenses from the beginning. The more you are willing to invest in editing, marketing and publicity, the more you will potentially sell. Be sure you set a realistic budget. Talk to your accountant about when you can or should start applying your tax write-offs against your sales.

Some counties or cities may require a business license. Where I live, it's an easy form at the county courthouse and approximately $20 a year. This action establishes my writing business as a sole proprietor, meaning I intend to make money with this venture, and I will pay the business taxes by running them through my personal taxes.

There are various legal categories describing what type of tax entity you can be, but I will leave that to the experts. I recommend A Writer's Legal Guide: An Authors Guild Desk Reference by Kay Murray and Tad Crawford. Although a book is also not a replacement for an attorney, it will give you some things to think about.

Once you have made it official, you are a writer. Now there are certain tax benefits that can arise from your status. Again, check with an accountant, but things like a computer, printer, office supplies and maybe even classes in your field may count as tax deductions. Purchasing this book should be a business expense. It's a rule of thumb that a business is expected to make money in three out of every five years, so you need to be serious in your endeavor. You don't have to be published to have tax write-offs, but you have to be actively trying.

You should also be diligent about record keeping, meetings you attend in relation to your writing and any submissions you make to a magazine or publisher. Even if you receive a "no thank you," you are showing intent to publish.

I would recommend setting up a professional email address (not SuzysMommy@gmail.com) to be used for business transactions, not personal email, to help keep your mailbox under control. Use this email address when signing up for newsletters or asking for price quotes for various services. It can be simple your firstname.lastname@. Or add "author" to the end of your name. If you have a website, you may be able to get an email through them. For example, mine is Dawn@DawnBrothertonAuthor.com.

Pull out your notebook.

How much money do you have to invest?

What will you use to track your business expenses and mileage?

Establish a business email account.

Does your city/county require a business license?

List 2-3 accountants (and their phone numbers) you would like to consult.

Writing Time

If this is your job, then treat it as such. Set aside time to write like you would any other profession. If it's a hobby, that's okay too, but then it isn't a business. Some swear by getting up and writing first thing in the morning. I am not a morning person, so staying up late works much better for me. My favorite time to write was after the kids went to bed, when the house was still and I had no demands pressing on me.

You need to find the time best for you. If you aren't sure, try a couple different times of the day. When do you feel the most creative? Where do you like to sit and work? Do you have a spot in the house that is your designated writing spot? Do you need to get out of the house? The library is usually a good place to let the muse overtake you. Some people are energized by the hustle and bustle of a coffee shop. Discover what's right for your rhythm.

Pull out your notebook.

Describe your ideal writing time.

Where is your ideal writing space?

What will you use to track your business expenses and mileage?

When will you apply for your business license?

List 2-3 accountants (and their phone numbers) you would like to consult.

Building Your Platform Now

In addition to practicing and treating your writing professionally, others need to know you are serious about being an author.

Whether you traditionally publish or self-publish, you will need a web presence. I suggest starting sooner rather than later. Having an established website, and perhaps a blog with followers, looks promising to an agent as you are sending out your query letters. It shows them you are taking your writing seriously enough to treat it as a business. If an agent is interested in you, trust me, they are going to check out your website, blog posts and social media pages. You really need a website. Then you need to be consistent and helpful.

Your platform is your contact base. Yes, it will start with friends and family, but hopefully, with the right attention, it will grow to reach your target audience. I'm no expert in this area so I'm going to suggest a few sites for you to check out. Brooke Warner on theWriteLife.com does a good job of getting you started. Brooke is founder of Warner Coaching Inc., publisher of She Writes Press, and author of What's Your Book? and How to Sell Your Memoir. She also sits on many boards of various publishing organizations.

You should separate your personal Facebook page where you post pictures of your kids and your dogs, from a professional author Facebook page where you stick to things dedicated to your writing. Of course, to build my following, I posted on my personal page for my friends and family to go follow my professional page. I just remind them not to post personal messages for me there. You need to start somewhere; let your friends and family help spread the word.

Joel Friedlander, owner of Marin Bookworks and Independent Publisher Book Award-winner for reference, provides some great advice on where to find free resources and information to get started in publishing (TheBookDesigner.com). He even offers a publication with self-publishing tips. I'll copy some resources here but go check out his full article.

Simon & Schuster Says Authors Should Blog and Social Network from Joanna Penn's The Creative Penn blog

The Dreaded Author's Platform by agent Rachelle Gardener

Welcome To Publetariat Vault University! by Indie Author April L. Hamilton

How to Build an Author Platform by author and Writer Mama Christina Katz

Building an Organic Web Presence by Marketing Maven Carol White

It's Not the Size of Your Platform, It's the Magic in It by Tribal Author Jonathan Fields

There are many different sites you can use to get started. But before you go there, let's go over some terminology to make it easier to follow their advice.

A domain name is the uniform resource locator, or url, of your website. Mine is www.Blue-Dragon-Publishing.com. I purchased it for at least a year. Companies that sell domains may offer discounts for two- or five-year terms. Some common sites to purchase domain names are GoDaddy, Google and WordPress. They are not the only ones, and I am not necessarily recommending them over any other. The purpose of this book is to help you on the road to publishing, so I am trying to give you a place to start looking. Shop around for the best price, but make sure you are getting a reputable company before turning over your credit card.

You'll find many endings to the domain name, ie, .com, .net, .org. Be realistic about what you purchase. Dot com is probably the most common in the United States, and you don't want to use .org if you aren't an organization. New domain endings are popping up all the time so research your options.

If you can get two similar urls for a good price, it may be worth it to own www.DawnBrothertonAuthor.com and www.DawnBrotherton.com. It increases the chances of people finding you. And it decreases the chances of others buying up a similar domain name and setting up a fake website to spoof people.

You don't need to set up multiple websites. Remember, a website is different than a domain name. The domain name points to your website.

Build one and point any other domain names you purchase to the website you have created. If you get stuck, your website provider's frequently asked questions or customer service can help you through this. It's very common.

After you own a domain name, build a website. You'll need a place to store the data or "host" it. Although it's possible to host on your own personal computer or server, it is highly discouraged. It's a safety nightmare. Select a company with cyber security in place, good customer service and back-ups for your site at least every few days.

If the thought of doing your own website is too daunting for you, there are many companies that will build one for you with a large variety of price tags. You may even be able to pay to have one set up and then you can take over maintenance and updates.

If you are working to establish a presence, the website will need all the standard items like your biography, published books and a link to where a fan can make a purchase.

If you are a self-published author or with a small press, I recommend selling books directly off your website, cutting out the middleman fees of a bookstore. There are many options for shopping carts. Check with your website host to see what is supported. PayPal is a very common shopping cart most people have heard of. Customers don't need to have a PayPal account to use the services. They can shop as a guest and pay with most major credit cards. There will be a service fee for any shopping cart you use. Some charge a monthly fee, where others are only per sale. If you are small, I recommend starting with the ones that charge per sale.

As you grow, your website should grow with you. You'll want to have a page where fans can find you to get an autograph at a book signing. Keep this current. It looks bad to have old news you are touting as "upcoming events."

Many authors have a blog—a regularly updated website or web page written in an informal or conversational style. You should aim for at least 300 words to help with search engine optimization (SEO). Blogs are a trend, and there's no telling how long they will last. If nothing else, for a writer, they're good practice. You can blog about almost anything. But just building it won't make them come. You need something to attract the types of readers who will be able to help your business (as a writer, in this case) grow. That may be other writers, readers, people who know readers, etc. It's all in how creative you are. If you're like me, it takes a while to get the hang of it.

You need the website and blog to be a part of your overall marketing plan, so they feed off each other. Your marketing plan will be touched on later.

Pull out your notebook.

What are some domain names you like? Think of variations in case the one you want is taken.

Where are you going to look to buy your domain name?

Set a goal to purchase your domain by a certain date.

Are you going to blog? If so, list at least ten topics to get you started. Read any good books lately? Start there.

Use some of the references above and take notes on their recommendations.

Chapter 4: Don't Rush to Publish

All of the things we have mentioned so far take time to set up, but it's worth doing it right the first time. Getting your manuscript ready for publishing will also take preparation.

Too many writers rush to publishing. It's such a great feeling to have your manuscript done, and you want to share it with the world as soon as possible.

Stop.

There are many more steps before it's time to submit for publishing.

I recommend you set your draft aside for a day or two. Celebrate the end of the draft writing stage and brace yourself for the editing phase. You personally should read through your finished manuscript a minimum of ten times. Yes, you read correctly—ten times. Look for different things each time.

Create a file with the description of each of your characters. In doing so, you will see if you are consistent, as well as determine if there is anything more you need to add to round out your characters.

> ➢ Did you describe each of the main characters?

> ➢ Have you built their backstories enough to make them believable, likeable and relatable?

> ➢ What is their flaw? Everyone has a flaw.

> ➢ How will they grow in character?

Are there any holes in reasoning with your plot? Have you ever read a book and said, "That would never happen?" You don't want people to say it about your book. Make sure the characters respond according to the personality you built for them.

Are there any words you can cut and tighten the story? Description is necessary; flowery words are not. Don't get carried away with -ly words—adverbs—in prose. If you are writing poetry, you want concise adjectives to paint a picture.

Where do you need to expand? Are you including all the essential information your reader needs to know? Did you leave something out because it's obvious to you as the writer? Your reader may not have the same background you have.

In my first book, The Obsession, I had to explain many military terms second-nature to me. I think in military time, so it didn't occur to me others didn't know what I was talking about until my sister asked a question after reading the first draft.

That's why you can never do a final edit on your own book. You know what you meant, so you may overlook something. Ask a trusted friend or spouse to read your story. Ask them to look for the same types of things—character development, holes in your story, gaps needing more explanation.

While this step is important and helpful, they are not playing the part of an editor. Someone close to you will have a hard time looking objectively at your work of art. They also know you well enough to know what you meant, even if it isn't what you said. Just like you will have a tendency to do, they will read into the story things that aren't really written there. But they can still help you move the project toward completion.

I also highly recommend writers' groups. Check with your local library or writers' organizations. Or start your own! These groups are made up of fellow writers who have the goal of improvement. Not all want to publish, but they should want honest, constructive feedback.

Determine a meeting schedule and hold each other accountable for work accomplished, giving your fellow writers incentive to take time for their craft. It will also help you get the feedback you need to improve. It has to be honest and complete feedback, or it doesn't do any good.

My group has made me rewrite sections when they don't flow well, gotten me to see things from another viewpoint and even helped me express the feelings of my characters with more detail. They have made me a much better writer. It's about content, flow and character enhancement.

You must be willing and able to provide honest feedback to your fellow group members, not only give platitudes to receive positive comments in exchange. Remember

the rule of the feedback sandwich—
positive, negative, positive. It's easier to
swallow.

Pull out your notebook.

Contact your local library about writers'
groups.

Do a search in your manuscript document
for unnecessary words to see if you use
them too often (ie. just, so, but, that and
-ly words). Replace where possible.

If you are writing a story with characters, create a file with a description of each one. Some people use notecards for this exercise.

Chapter 5: Editing

When you think your manuscript is as clean as possible, there are still a few more steps. Don't rush through any of this—it'll pay off in the long run.

No matter how good of a writer you are, you need an editor (or editors!). Don't fool yourself.

As a start-up, you'll be tempted to do the economical thing, which means doing everything yourself. There are some things that can be done on your own, and some things I would highly recommend getting someone else to do. You can NOT edit your own work! Trust me, I tried and failed miserably. I have been an executive officer numerous times in the Air Force, and I pride myself on my ability to catch typos and misplaced commas. It is totally different when it's your own work. You read what you meant to write, not necessarily what you wrote. I had my sister, who is a teacher, proofread it, only to find out later she felt bad about picking at my work, so she held back on me.

You may be asking, "Doesn't the publisher pay for the editing?" Yes, they might—if your manuscript is in good enough shape to make it through the proposal process. The publisher needs to know you are a serious writer who puts in the extra effort to come up with a solid draft. You have one chance to make a first impression, so get it edited. Besides, you learn something from every editor, improving your writing in the process.

Types of Editors

Whether you plan on submitting to a publisher, or especially if you are self-publishing, you should invest in a professional editor. An editor has been trained to look for certain things in a manuscript and to help shape it into a sellable book. They are typically well-versed in the style guide appropriate for various works. Chicago Manual of Style is used most often for novels. This book is the go-to for editors and a great resource for writers, as well. Nonfiction editors tend to use the

Associated Press Stylebook. Poetry editors may use a different style guide.

Editors often times will specialize in types of books. A reader for textbooks may not be the best one for a fiction novel. Choose wisely.

There are multiple stages of editing. You will hear them described in a variety of ways, but this is the basic gist.

➢ Developmental: Big picture

➢ Line Editing: Language-use

➢ Copy Editing: Grammar police

➢ Fact checker: Checks your resources

➢ Proofreading: Last look before printing

The developmental editor will focus on the big picture. Is the dialogue believable? Have the characters been developed fully? Do the plot twists have something to back them up, or do they come out of nowhere? Is it engaging? Does it pull the reader along, making them unable to put your book down?

This next stage is line editing. Line editing will focus on creative content, writing style, and language-use at the sentence and paragraph level. Much more attention will be applied to the way you use language to communicate your story to the reader. Is your language clear, fluid and pleasurable to read? Does it convey a sense of atmosphere, emotion and tone? Are you using broad generalizations and clichés? Have you overused an uncommon word?

Copy editing is next and is more detailed-oriented. Grammar, punctuation and consistency in formatting are examples of a few things this editor is looking for. This person is like an English teacher on steroids. They practically have the style guide memorized, or at least know when they need to look something up. It's amazing the minutiae good editors know about things most people couldn't put their finger on but can sense when something isn't quite right.

Some copy editors will distinguish between light, medium and heavy editing—and the price point may vary. Light copyediting checks basic spelling, grammar, punctuation and formatting. Medium will also look at parallel sentence structure, correct passive voice and give extra attention to character traits and setting.

Heavy copyediting has also been referred to as the slash method. This editor looks for places to cut to give your finished product a smooth flow. Don't despair. They may also recommend additions in certain areas needing more definition.

Make sure to finish line editing before beginning copy editing. You don't want to pay for copy editing and then change things significantly through line editing. Make sure to ask when you are hiring someone what they specialize in. Often it's good to have two different editors for this process.

If you are writing nonfiction, you may also need a fact checker. This person double checks your references, makes sure they are cited correctly and proper permissions have been granted to use the quotes or opinions. As you can imagine, this is a labor-intensive, but often necessary, step. It is very important when writing nonfiction to ensure you have documented all your sources and you're very organized. That will make this step go much quicker.

Proofreading is generally the last step. It's also one of the hardest because you are so close you can taste the joys your royalties are going to buy. But again, I caution you not to rush. At this point you will have a physical copy in your hands. This is your last chance to catch typos, poor margins, line breaks and the quality of pictures. Take your time and read your story again. Better yet, have someone else with a critical eye read it. You can pay an editor to do this final check, or you can take it upon yourself. As a publisher, I always put the proof copy in the hands of the author.

Pull out your notebook.

List options for writers' groups in your area.

Who do you trust to read your draft?

What local organizations exist to help you on your journey?

Hiring an Editor

Prepare yourself for sticker shock, because editing is expensive. I won't say whether or not I think editors are worth what they charge, but I will say they are necessary. And you get what you pay for. If you pay nothing for editing, that may be all it's worth.

Request a sample edit before you hire an editor. You need to know how the editor operates, if they are responsive, and if your personalities are compatible. You are trusting this person with your baby. You need to have confidence in them and feel comfortable leaving your work in their hands.

Send out samples to a few different editors (sometimes they specify first chapter, so many words, etc.) and see how quickly they respond and whether or not you like how they interact with you. If they take too long, or their comments are snippy, you may want to consider a different editor. You need to establish a bond with your editor, so be sure it's going to work.

I like working with Microsoft Word track changes. Then I can see exactly what changes the editor is suggesting and easily accept or reject their suggestions. Most editors and publishers I know use Microsoft Word, so this feature is definitely worth taking the time to get to know.

It's very common for line and copy editors to charge by the word. Because there are so many different fonts, margins and layout styles, charging by the page isn't always practical. If you are using Microsoft Word, it's easy to get a word count by looking in the bottom, left-hand side of the screen. Editors' fees will vary greatly—anything from two cents a word to five cents. For example, a 90,000-word novel (standard for trade fiction) could run you between $1,800 and $4,500. Take a deep breath, though, and let the sticker shock pass. If your work is in good shape with only minor formatting to be corrected, an editor may give you a better price.

It does add up quickly though—another reason it behooves you to write as tight as possible before sending it out for editing.

You don't have to agree with everything the editor says—or like it. Sometimes the truth hurts, and you won't like it. You have to step away from your labor of love and try to be objective about the comments being offered. At this stage in the game, you are still in control. You can choose to accept or reject the recommendations made.

Let me give you an example. In my second Jackie Austin book, I used too many military terms that were perfectly natural to me and made sense the way I wrote them. The suggestion was I needed to explain more and use different terms. I felt it would detract from the military feel. I stepped back and looked at it from an outsider's perspective, and the editor was spot on. It took a while to rework the wording so we were both happy with it.

In my most recent Lady Tigers Series book, which is a youth fiction story about a girls' fastpitch softball team, the editor (a different one) said I had to add a boy character into the storyline or boys wouldn't read it. I'm writing a sports' series for young ladies; there are plenty of sports' books for boys. I did not add a male character.

There are multiple options to search for an editor. Writers' magazines and the internet are full of advertisements. Don't jump at the first one you see. If you have writer friends, ask them for recommendations—learn from their mistakes. If you belong to a writers' organization (like Sisters in Crime, Chesapeake Bay Writers, etc.), tap into their vast contact base.

Don't think you're getting a deal by going with the lowest quote. The editors with the most experience tend to charge a lot more because they can. They have an established clientele who value their work and can afford their prices. If you are just starting out, you may not be ready for them, unless money is no object.

You want to ensure the terms of your agreement up front. Is the price you're paying for one read-through only? Or are you going to exchange emails until it's done? Or somewhere in between?

It's important to have something in writing so there's no confusion later to cause hard feelings. Email documentation may be fine, although some prefer to have a contract in place. Paying half of the editor's fee up front is perfectly acceptable, but I recommend holding off on final payment until work is delivered. Make sure you agree on a deadline and have the terms spelled out describing what happens if the deadline is missed.

Once you have emailed your precious work of art to an editor, be patient and give him time to do a good job. Ensure you work the editing piece into your timeline. You will feel rushed because, now that you're done, you want to see your writing in print. Good editing takes time. You've done your job. Allow your editor a solid 30 days (depending on the complexity and length of your manuscript) to do his.

When the Edits Come Back

When the edits come back, grab your favorite beverage, find a quiet place to read, and take a few deep breaths. Now, absorb what has been given to you. Although painful at the time, I have learned a lot from my editors and am more mindful not to make the same mistakes twice. The more I write, the fewer edits are needed. It's a really good feeling.

If the edits are simple grammar and commas, you should be able to accept track changes and be on to your next stage. If they are more substantial comments, you may need to set them aside, let the ideas seep into your subconscious before you attack the re-write a few days later. If you have questions about the inputs your editor has given you, go back and ask for clarification before you start rewriting.

Turn on track changes so your editor can see what you changed and won't have to re-read the whole manuscript.

Chapter 6: Publishing Options

I never truly understood why publishers take such a large portion of the profits from your book until I got into the publishing side of this business. Now it makes so much more sense to me.

Each publisher is different, and each contract may have its own nuances. But, think about it: a full-service publisher is paying for all levels of editing, cover design, book design, marketing (albeit often not much in that area), printing, warehousing, fulfillment, and distribution. The cost will quickly add up when you try to set up those activities on your own.

We'll break down these functions in more detail later. For now, let's talk about publishing options.

Vanity   Hybrid
_____

        Self   Traditional

Vanity Press

A vanity press is an organization that will take whatever you give them, make copies or prints for you, bind it to look like a book, and call it a book. They charge large sums of money, and you get very little for the cost—a few copies and maybe a poster. They prey on people who are rushing to the end product without any real desire for quality. These writers only want to be able to say they published a book. If there wasn't a market for it, vanity presses wouldn't exist. If you are a serious writer, avoid these enterprises.

_____

Pull out your notebook.

What appeals to you about this method?

What's the downside?

_____

Traditional Publishing

At the other extreme are the traditional publishers. Think HarperCollins, Scholastic and Penguin-Random House. There is nothing wrong with this model, and it has served readers and writers for many years, and they will be around for many years to come. Think back to your goals. If it was to get rich, a big publisher is not a guarantee.

Do an internet search on "What percentage of authors are successful" to get the most current statistics. It's eye-opening. Even traditional authors are rolling the dice as to whether or not they have found the latest, hottest book. According to a Publishers' Weekly blog post dated February 2015, of 50 books published, only 1 or 2 will break out. Between 20-30 may hit the break-even point.

Traditional publishing is a money-making business, and they will do their best to make money—for you as well as for themselves.

There is some thought that if you sign with a traditional publisher, your contract will come with a large advance. Not so much the case anymore. Budget cuts are everywhere, including with publishers. And even if you do get an advance, it is an advance payment of royalties they expect you to earn over the life of your book. You won't start collecting royalty payments until your book breaks even in cost, and the publisher has collected back your advance. Then you will begin to collect your approximately 10% of the profit, minus your agent's fees, of course.

Agents are a must when dealing with larger traditional publishers as are found in New York City. It's an agent's job to look out for your best interests. After all, they only make money if you make money.

Be careful what you wish for. I've heard it said if a writer decides to go with a traditional publisher, it may be the last decision she ever makes...because the publisher will take over from there. Be very careful (and consult an attorney) before signing a contract. For example, you may end up signing away your right to cover design and title. If you aren't careful, you may also lose your foreign sales and movie rights. If this sounds daunting, you need an attorney.

Typical shelf-life of a book is three months, meaning. it usually doesn't stay on the bookstore shelf longer than that. By then, if it hasn't caught fire, it probably won't, so not much money is spent on marketing. At which point, a publisher may decide to keep it on the back burner. If they hold the rights, there isn't anything you can do about it. They may decide not to warehouse for bookstores, which basically means your book goes out of print. The good news is, in the digital age, nothing needs to truly go out of print.

Even if your title is getting no love from the big guys, you may have signed away your rights and may not be able to sell it on your own. In essence, it's no longer yours. Depending on the wording in your contract, you may not even be able to resurrect the same characters for another novel. Read your contract carefully. Are you sensing a theme?

Traditional publishers, and even some bigger indie presses, tend to follow the fads. Ever notice when one vampire book hits it big, vampires invade our bookstores? Then they will fade away (as vampires should), and some other excitement will hit the stands. Maybe witches, demons or robots.

If you're a writer who can write quickly and on any issue in style at the moment, it might work fine for you. Most writers have a passion for certain genres or topics. It's hard to stop everything that has been building up in their mind waiting to find its way to paper for the chance of rising above the throng of writers chasing the fad.

I know this is going to sound like I'm contradicting myself after saying publishers follow the fads, but there is the other side that is slow and methodical about the book choices they put out. The same publisher doesn't want to put out two books about an airplane crash to compete with each other. Even if both books are equally awesome, they are more likely to spread them apart by a publishing cycle. So your fantastic tale may be scheduled to release one to two years later than you had hoped. Meanwhile, start your next book.

It sounds like I have been bashing traditional publishing, which was not the intent of the previous section. Honestly, it goes back to the beginning when I asked you the question: Why are you writing? If your goal is to be signed by one of the top five publishers, then whether your book takes two years or three to hit the stands, it doesn't matter; you have accomplished your goal.

But you have alternatives.

Pull out your notebook.

What appeals to you about this method?

What's the downside?

Self-Publishing

The great thing about self-publishing is anyone can do it. The problem with self-publishing is anyone can do it.

When done right, it is a great alternative. Sadly, too many people have written something at midnight, determined it was great on first draft, and slapped it up on Amazon the next morning. No editing, no formatting, no proofreading. You will understand what I'm talking about if you've ever purchased one of these books. It's disappointing and a waste of money. I even read one where the authors simply put a disclaimer in it along the lines of, "We know there are errors, so don't bother commenting about them on the reviews."

Uh? How are you supposed to take someone seriously who cannot be bothered to correct known mistakes? And in the digital age, those are easy to fix.

If you are a serious writer, then take the time to make your work readable. You probably spent countless hours on your book (or years, as in my case). Spend a little more time and make it fit for the public. I beg you not to cut corners. I will give you suggestions on how you can save money in certain places, but there are some places worth spending money on. Editors are one of those places, as previously discussed.

There are some good points to self-publishing. You are on your own timeline. If you cram hard enough, you can turn your book much quicker than the one to two years a traditional publisher may take once a contract has been signed. For example, you aren't as worried about competing with yourself on a similar title coming out at the same time. And all your energy and focus can be on producing the one title.

It will take considerable time and energy, though. As we will discuss, a lot of steps go into publishing, and some things you don't know you don't know.

Another point on the good side: once you have expended energy, you aren't sharing your profits with agents and publishers. You will, of course, have to pay the bills for editing, cover, printing and marketing, but the final product is yours for all time. Don't forget to copyright it! We'll talk about that soon.

You call the shots. The cover is the way you like it. The title is what you always dreamed it would be, and you can name your characters whatever you want. It's an amazing feeling… but do some research to make sure you aren't shooting yourself in the foot by doing it your way. It's worth knowing the trends and understanding why certain things are taking off while other topics are dying on the vine.

A downside to self-publishing is you won't have the reach a traditional publishing house can give you. Libraries typically won't buy a self-published book and getting a Library of Congress number is tough without a publisher.

With the advent of digital printing, print-on-demand (POD) printers are popping up all over the internet. Do your homework and see what you're getting for your money.

Print-on-demand means a book is only printed when needed. If someone buys your book from a POD printer, one book is printed and shipped to the customer. You had no upfront printing or warehousing cost. Of course, the printing cost will be much higher than doing a traditional print run. In a print run, the more books you buy, the less the price per book is.

After the POD company charges you for the cost of printing, and the seller takes their processing fee (approximately 33-50% depending on many factors), you need to ensure what you charged the customer was high enough to cover those costs and enough for you to make a profit. In order to stay competitively priced with like-books, you will probably find your profit margin is very small.

If you decide to go with a print run of 200-1,000 books, you'll probably get a better printing price, but you need to front the cost, to warehouse them and to ship them yourself or pay someone else to warehouse and ship for you. We will cover warehousing and fulfillment in more detail when we expand the self-publishing things to know.

Some things are harder to come by in self-publishing, but they may not be important to you. Distributors, for example, are hard for an independent publisher to get—I've never heard of a self-published author who had a traditional distributor. That doesn't mean it can't happen if you are willing to pay the price. See Chapter 13 for more details.

Another advantage to self-publishing is you maintain your rights. If your book does go viral on social media, you will have the rights to broker a movie deal.

Pull out your notebook.

What appeals to you about this method?

What's the downside?

Indie Publishing

Independent publishing (or indie press) is becoming more common. Smaller presses with less staff are standing up every day and providing a great alternative for writers who want to focus on writing and leave more of the business end to someone else. But there are drawbacks to indies as well.

Some of the good things first: you don't have to reinvent the wheel. There are plenty of people out there who have already figured out how to navigate the ins and outs of publishing.

The indie publishers typically have accounts and credibility already established with the Library of Congress, the federal copyright office and various online sales channels. They know where to purchase the international standard book numbers required and can probably get them cheaper than if you purchased them yourself. They will save you from making the mistakes they made. Is that worth your time and money?

An Indie will have established relationships with printers, editors, cover artists, book designers, and more, saving you the time of having to search and vet them.

Often, independent publishers can edit and format your manuscript faster and get it into the market a lot quicker than a traditional publisher. In addition, because the indie publisher's scale of published works is much smaller, they don't have as many topics to deconflict within a publishing cycle.

Because they are independent, almost every indie publisher will have set up their business in a way that makes the most sense for them. The good news for you is if you look hard enough, you should be able to find someone who will fit your needs as well. Indies vary greatly in the level of support they provide and amount of money you have to invest. You need to run the numbers and see what is most advantageous to your life situation.

Now, on the negative side, indie presses usually don't have a large reach. Getting books into libraries and bookstores take the work of distributors, warehouses and fulfillment offices. Big publishing houses can afford to outsource those items; smaller publishers usually cannot. They will rely on Amazon as the main sales venue, using a company like Ingram to make titles available to bookstores and libraries. But unless the publisher pays extra, Ingram distribution is simply your title in a list of many titles, with no agent actually pushing it for you. Still better than nothing, and at least a bookstore can order it if a customer walks in their door and asks for it.

There are some companies calling themselves distributors for independent presses, but really, they are print-on-demand companies putting your title in a digital catalog along with thousands of other unknown authors. These catalogs are available for libraries and booksellers.

A traditional distributor takes an interest in the titles they carry and is the author's advocate for sales. Remember, the more they sell, the more money they make.

If you pay extra, smaller distributors will give you more room in their magazine and on the website, but they are still not an advocate for your title because they have other independents as well. Their priority is measured by the amount of money their client will pay for advertising. There's nothing wrong with that model. You just need to understand the model you are paying for.

Pull out your notebook.

What appeals to you about this method?

What's the downside?

Do you have money to invest upfront for a print run?

Are you the type who needs to control every part of the process?

Is your time worth the money you would pay someone else to do some of the work?

Chapter 7: Query Letters

If you are going to go the traditional publishing route, you will need to do a query letter, either for an agent or a publisher. Even if you decide to self-publish or use an independent publisher, it is good practice to write a query letter.

For fiction, typically the manuscript will need to be complete before you begin to query. If you get a response from an agent asking for the manuscript, you want to be able to reply quickly, before they move on to someone else.

For nonfiction, a detailed outline, including 200-300 words describing each chapter, is a common requirement, along with at least one completed chapter as a sample of your writing style. This is referred to as a Book Proposal.

Research

Spend time in bookstores scouring the shelves for books in the same genre as yours. Check the inside cover for the publishing house and take note. Make sure you collect quite a few. Do they have an imprint? An imprint is a division within the publishing house focusing on a particular genre.

While you're there, check the copyright page and acknowledgement and see if the author thanks his or her agent. Capture that name as well.

This is where the internet has made your job much easier than writers of the past had it. Get to a computer and look up the publishing house, searching for the specific editor who covers your genre. A query letter has a better chance of getting through to the reader if you take the time to address it directly to the right person. The publisher's website will also tell you whether or not you need an agent to apply, or if they will accept manuscripts directly from authors. Smaller publishing houses may accept submissions without an agent. Larger houses count on agents to weed out works not quite ready and requiring developmental work.

Another book widely recommended is The Writers' Market. It's a good tool, but I find it overwhelming and daunting just looking at the thickness. Some people swear by it. I recommend getting a copy from your local library first to see if it's worth your investment. It is updated every year.

Once you have identified which publisher you want to send a query letter to, make sure you check the agent or publisher's website for the exact format they require. If you don't follow what they ask for, they may disregard your query letter without reading. If you can't follow instructions, they probably don't want to work with you.

Pull out your notebook.

What publishers handle the genre you are writing?

Do they have a specific imprint for it?

Go to their website.

What are their requirements?

Do you need an agent?

Basic Requirements

I always struggled with query letters because they feel like I'm selling myself—which is the purpose. Or more accurately, a query letter is to sell your writing.

All agents or publishers will probably require a few basic things, so you can put together a template and tailor each letter depending on who you are submitting to.

- ➢ Facts: Your genre, word count, title and subtitle

- ➢ Hook: the meat of the query in 100-200 words

- ➢ Bio: if you are published, say so. If not, don't mention it. Why are you the best one to write this story? Have you won awards?

- ➢ Personalization: Why did you pick this agent? Did you meet somewhere? Are you a fan of a particular author they worked with?

- ➢ Thank you and closing: Include how they can reach you

Jane Friedman has over 20 years of experience in the book and magazine publishing industry. She has a blog to help writers and does a great job of outlining a query letter:

https://janefriedman.com/query-letters/

Follow the steps Friedman outlines, then have others proof your query letter for you, preferably before they've read your story. What you want to know is if it gets them interested in reading more. They have to be brutally honest with you or it won't be effective. Make your query letter concise, without fluffy words.

Your query letter should have a hook giving the sense of the protagonist, the dilemma he or she is in, choices to be made, and what makes your book stand out—all this without giving up the ending. The hook should leave the reader wanting more, and the agent asking for a synopsis (in which you will have to give up the ending).

I would be wary of online ads that say they can write a great query letter for you for $xxx. If the query letter is supposed to be a sample of your writing, having someone else write it for you seems like cheating. Besides, as painful as it may seem, you will learn a lot from writing it yourself. You will learn to be succinct, which is the beginning of your elevator pitch (which we discuss in Chapter 9). It will also highlight where you may be lacking and need to improve upon.

Pull out your notebook.

Write the template of your query letter to include your bio, hook and book information.

Get at least two other people to proof it for you.

Chapter 8: Agents

Some publishers won't talk to you without an agent. Agents have contacts with various publishing circles and pitch your manuscript to publishers on your behalf. The better deal they get for you, typically the more money they make, so they are motivated to get you as much as they can. Often, they also negotiate a contract for you. New writers will at times jump at the first offer from a publisher because they're excited to get noticed. Agents help keep it real for you.

Getting the right agent is crucial to your success. If you enter into a contract with her, it will be a long-term commitment so think long and hard (and consult an attorney) before signing any documents. Even some of the smaller publishers may require an agent.

Like publishing imprints, agents typically have certain genres they specialize in, because that's where their connections are. Pick one who fits your style. And make sure you click with your agent. It will be a close relationship, so you have to be ready for the long-haul.

Keep in mind every layer you add between you and your published book will be that much less money you get to pocket. Most writers aren't in the business to get rich (although who would complain?). With the expansion of indie presses, the need for an agent is not as great as it once was. Many independent publishers will consider you even without an agent. But make sure you have someone knowledgeable read the fine print on the contract before you sign it.

Where to Find an Agent

There are so many authors and so many agents in the world, you will hear various stories on how they got together. Very few luck into it. It takes research, dedication and a good product. Here are a few examples of where you may find an agent.

> ➤ Writing Conferences

> ➤ Online Search

> ➤ Twitter

- Book Acknowledgements
- MS Wishlist
- Chuck Sambuchino
- QueryTracker
- Association of Author Representatives

Many writing conferences will invite agents, and attendees are given 15 minutes to make their pitch and try to capture the attention of an agent.

You can search online. Check out any potentials carefully. Talk to others they represent, if at all possible. See if any of their writers have written nice things about them in their acknowledgements or on their websites.

If you follow certain organizations or people on Twitter, they will sometimes tweet when they are looking for new clients, writers or poets. Here are a few to try: @poetswritersinc, @writersdigest, @submittable. This is NOT AN ENDORSEMENT of any of the above. I only mention they do post calls for writers. Check out any group you deal with carefully and ask for references.

One of the best places to look is at a bookstore. A bookstore is better than a library in this case because you will get the people who are current. Go to the section of your bookstore where your book would be shelved. Take note of the publishers who handle your genre. Look at the copyright page. Sometimes an editor or agent is listed there. Also look on the acknowledgement page to see if the author thanked his or her literary agent. Jot down the name of the person and the agency. Make sure you note which book it came from. It'll be helpful when writing the query letter.

Chuck Sambuchino is a freelance editor and was named by Forbes as a top publishing influencer on twitter. His website has many resources great for a young writer. He introduces new agents who are looking for writers to represent.

There is a website called QueryTracker.net with a free and a paid, upgraded version to help you find a literary agent. You can add criteria to narrow your search and then use the software to keep track of who you queried and when, so you remember to follow up with them.

MS Wishlist is another place to look for an agent: http://mswishlist.com/mswl. This is a database where you can sort by genre.

You should always crosscheck with the Association of Author Representatives http://aaronline.org/ to make sure your potential agent is registered and not a fly-by-night person trying to make a fast buck. Most agents only make money if you are making money, giving them the incentive to work hard to sell your manuscript. The 2018 going rate is 15% of royalties received.

You still need to do your research and be realistic. The well-known agents are looking for well-known authors, or at least ones they feel will make them a lot of money. New agents who are willing to take a chance on you are worth more than the agents who won't even look in your direction. Just think, maybe you can come to fame together!

Pull out your notebook.

Create a spreadsheet or similar to help track your agent submissions.

List the contact information for at least five agents you will target.

Research an agent to learn something personable you can add to your query letter to catch their attention.

List writers' conferences realistic for you to attend where agents are invited.

Chapter 9: Publicity vs. Marketing

There is a difference between marketing and publicity, although they are often confused. Marketing focuses on the message you want to get out about your book via advertisements, radio, TV and newspapers—even blogs. Publicity is when other people are talking about your book. A publicist is paid to pitch your books to magazines, TV, radio, etc. to get reviews. They don't pay for good reviews, just the attention you need for your book to be reviewed in the first place.

Marketing

And what good are the reviews if you aren't marketing them? Marketing and publicity go hand-in-hand. Talk to your publicist and get recommendations on the best venues to market that will blend well with your publicity plan. Marketing is typically about the book you're selling now. Hopefully your campaign will bring in dedicated readers for the long haul, but the real focus is now and getting your cover in front of as many people as your budget will allow.

You need to create a marketing plan. There are many online classes and books to walk you through this. Again, if you aren't interested in doing it yourself, you can hire an expert. A marketing plan will be like a calendar where you decide what to release to what audience at what time.

You need to build up to your book release and then continue at least six months after. Choreographing newspaper interviews, radio spots, flyers, internet blog tours, advertisements and social media pushes to get the most bang for your buck is truly an art form. You should start laying out your plan before your book is even finished; I would suggest by the time you have your first draft completed.

Let's talk about a few ways to market inexpensively:

- ➢ Website
- ➢ Local library
- ➢ Donate to fundraiser

➤ Networking groups

Your website will be key to marketing. If someone hears about you on the radio and it piques their interest, chances are they will do an internet search for you. If you don't have a healthy website, you'll lose them, and your advertising money will have been wasted.

For some free advertising, try donating to your local library. Sometimes they will put your name and picture in the newspaper to thank you.

Also, support a good cause by donating your book to a fundraiser. Make sure to provide them a blurb for their advertising, and if the book will be displayed, ask if you can put out extra business cards or bookmarkers next to the display that anyone interested may pick up. Again, you won't necessarily see a direct return on investment, but getting your name out helps. Discuss with your tax consultant, because donations to a nonprofit may also be deductible—typically only for the cost of producing the book.

Networking groups are everywhere. Find one that makes sense to you. If you are in business and are using this book as support for your company, networking should fit in nicely. Remember, networking groups are about helping each other's businesses, so don't go just expecting to sell your book and then move on. Through these groups, you may find other speaking engagements.

It does take money to make money, so be sure you budget for marketing. In a Jane Friedman blog about marketing and publicity (https://janefriedman.com /difference-marketing-publicity/), she discusses some interesting statistics. One I found to be a huge eye opener is that 95% of all bestselling books had more than $50,000 spent on their marketing and public relations.

I don't know about you, but I don't have $50,000 to spend right now on marketing. I will be happy with what my budget can buy.

Learn a lesson from me: don't sprinkle your marketing money around. If you are going to do it, do it right. Various marketing techniques concentrated over the same period will get you a larger return.

Pull out your notebook.

Brainstorm ideas where you can market your work inexpensively.

What social media avenues can you use?

What organizations are you involved with? Is there an opportunity to donate a book to their cause?

How much money do you have budgeted for marketing?

Publicity

Most large publishing houses will have an in-house publicist, but his or her attention is stretched thin between many authors. It doesn't hurt to have your own publicist focusing on you. You only have one chance for a first release. But brace yourself—this is another investment in your future. The standard fee in the U.S. is about $100 an hour. You should count on, at the minimum, 50 hours to start. It sounds daunting, but you're paying for their contacts and know-how. There's no direct correlation between your output and how many books you will sell; don't believe it if a publicist tries to make you any guarantees. Publicity is focused on the long-term. Although a campaign may be centered around a certain title, publicity will usually focus more attention on the author rather than the single title. A new release is an excuse to talk more about the author.

If you are going to do the work yourself, there are reputable companies you can pay to review your work. Again, no guarantee it will be a positive review, but it will get read. Kirkus is one of the most well-known and charge upward of $400 to read your book. And I warn you now, they can be brutal, but a positive word from them is like gold to the libraries. You have to have tough skin. Foreword Reviews is the same type of service. They will consider reviewing it for free if you get the final, polished version to them four months prior to publication. Or you can pay for a review for $499 (at the time of this publication). For $695, you can get two reviews.

I'm not advocating for these companies in particular or any companies like these. I only give them as examples that you can pay to have a reputable company review your work if you aren't interested in hiring a publicist, but it's still expensive.

Other chances for publicity and reviews you can manage yourself include writing contests and giveaways. Not all contests are created equally, and you shouldn't have to pay much to enter a contest. If you search, there are free contests or those with a nominal fee (less than $100). Check out all your options before you throw money at different venues. What will you get for your money? Feedback? Reviews? Ask around and make sure the company is sound and not a scam. How long have they been around? Have you heard of them before? Do professional writing organizations endorse them?

Goodreads, now owned by Amazon, is a free online community providing opportunities for book reviews and making suggestions for books based on your past reading history. They host book giveaways for a fee. You post your title with Goodreads, they select the winners of the giveaway, you mail it out, and the reader provides a review. Caution, you may want to limit the members who can apply for your giveaway. My first time, I left it open, and it cost me a small fortune to mail books overseas.

If you are writing for children or young adults, see if you can get a librarian or teacher to write a review for your website and marketing material. If your book is nonfiction, ask an expert in the field to give you a blurb.

Bottom line is you want to come up with a plan that includes both marketing and publicity and fits your budget. Be realistic in your expectations. Your first time out, you are laying the foundation. With your next book or next push, the foundation will grow along with name recognition. This is a long-distance race, not a sprint.

Pull out your notebook.

What blogs do you follow? Do they do book reviews?

What is the process to submit a news release to your local newspaper(s)?

Draft a news release. Search the internet for examples.

Selling Yourself

I was at a book festival and one writer (not published yet) stopped by to chat. He told me he "didn't want to do all this stuff," gesturing at the number of authors who had gathered to sell their books. I had to break it to him that selling books face-to-face is the way an author makes the most money! Cut out the middleman storekeeper or online retailer, and you will have more money in your pocket.

Not to mention, you're getting your name known by a larger audience. Even if people don't buy your book there, they saw your table or presentation at the book festival, store or signing. The next time they're looking for something to read, they may remember seeing you and be curious enough to go in search of one of your books. They may mention to a friend they met you at an event. Word of mouth is a great advertising tool.

Even with the traditional publishers, the author is expected to market his or her book. It's the same with musicians, painters and other artists. The publisher wants to see what you're doing to promote your name and your product. I realize many authors prefer to hide behind a keyboard, but that isn't the world of business. To be successful, you need to let people know you are successful.

You should always be your biggest advocate. You can do this without sounding pretentious or over-confident. When people ask what you do, tell them you are a writer. Be prepared for the follow-up questions: "What's the title of your book, and where can I get it?" To avoid any awkwardness if you haven't yet been published, most people say they are a writer until their first book gets published, at which time you're considered an author. This is not a hard and fast rule; just a rule of thumb.

It took me a long time to get used to saying I was an author. Now I still struggle with the question, "How many books have you sold?" To me, that's a very personal question, like asking, "How much money do you make?" I try to dodge it by saying I write for the love of writing. Or I say I'm not losing money.

Pull out your notebook.

Do a search for book festivals within a radius you are willing to travel. Most book up to six months in advance. Download the application.

What other festivals are available? Craft festivals? Local independent bookstores?

How will you answer when people ask what you do for a living?

Elevator Speech

You've probably heard the term elevator pitch before, or you may have heard it called a logline. It isn't just for writers. It's for anyone trying to sell themselves or a product. If you're in an elevator with someone, and they ask what you do for a living, you only have the 30 seconds it takes to ride the elevator to hook them. If you have multiple books, you need different speeches to fit the occasion.

When people ask what my kids' series is about, I answer with my tagline. "It's about a fast-pitch softball team where the girls learn that being part of a team is about more than what happens on the field."

I add it's a ten-part series focusing on different issues third and fourth graders are interested in such as lying, bullying, separation, etc. Usually folks will ask questions, and I can expand on some of the topics addressed.

If there's more time, follow up with the quick summary—one or two sentences to explain the main character and the conflict for your novel. WHO, WHAT, WHEN, WHERE, and WHY.

How is my series different? What makes it stand out? Many sports books have been written for middle grade, but they tend to focus on boys' sports. This one is about a girls' team.

An elevator pitch format may vary between a novel and a nonfiction book. The important thing is to get the message across in a short period of time.

Write out a few versions of your elevator speech and practice in front of a mirror. Then step it up by talking to a spouse, child or friend. It must sound natural. Don't try to use flowery words or sound stiff. That's a dead giveaway you are delivering a pitch rather than having a conversation.

An elevator speech will come in handy if you happen to run into an agent or publisher at a party, wedding or Sunday picnic. Or, after your novel is in print (or on eBook), this is your chance to sell a few more books. Word-of-mouth starts with YOU!

Pull out your notebook.

Draft your elevator pitch using this format:

A (insert adjective) (insert profession or social role) must (insert goal, may include the timeline or stakes).

Now play with your draft until it feels comfortable.

Write an extended version in case you are given more time.

Chapter 10: Selling Your Story

There are many options for getting your books into readers' hands. You will make more money per book on face-to-face sales but selling takes times away from writing. You can leave the sales up to another venue, but then you share your profits with them.

Bookstores are the most traditional option, although Amazon is the forerunner for book sales. Don't forget libraries. EBooks can be a very cost-effective option sold in multiple places and also used in libraries.

Brick-n-Mortar

Set your expectations realistically. Shelf life in a bookstore is short (approximately three months). Without a salesperson and a huge following to ensure your books don't get returned, I would recommend avoiding the large chain bookstores. If you are determined to be in a brick and mortar store, visit your local independent bookstores.

Most bookstores will require a 45-55% discount, and the store holds all the cards. They can order and return books to the distributor at will. The "seller," in our case the self-published author or independent publisher, is responsible for the cost of all returns—the price the store paid for the book, reshipping and restocking fees. Then the store can turn around and reorder the same books they returned the day prior. I don't believe this ever happens willfully or with spite; more through carelessness and no checks and balances.

In most cases, you have to work through a distributor. If you are using IngramSpark as a POD, you are covered. If not, you also have to pay a separate warehouse or fulfillment center (see Chapter 13). Even if it is your neighborhood bookstore and you can walk books into them, many of the chains require the use of a distributor because it's easier for billing purposes. If you are going to the store for a book signing, many stores still require the use of the distributor and will not let you walk away with the leftover books—they charge you to mail them back to the distributor, who will then charge you restocking fees. If you are printing 10,000+ books, perhaps these numbers don't concern you, but for the majority of authors starting out, those costs can be daunting.

Independent bookstores are worth discussing separately. There is an independent bookstore association (IndieBound.org) to help an author locate independent bookstores worth approaching. Keep in mind, they will also need the 55% discount in order to make money. Many of them also require a distributor for ease of billing. Some are hesitant to work directly with authors because there is no perceived quality control, but at times, they will work with smaller publishers to show support for indies.

Read the bookstores' websites carefully before approaching them. I have found some state quite plainly if you sell on Amazon, don't bother approaching them.

That brings us to the elephant in the room— Amazon. Amazon has the reach allowing self-published authors and independent publishers to flourish. They still take their percentage upon the sale, but depending on which model you elect, you can save on distributor costs and act as your own fulfillment agency. But bookstores typically won't purchase through the Amazon distribution arm because the books are non-returnable. You can (and I recommend) sell on Amazon as well as having a distributor like IngramSpark.

Amazon

Like it or not, Amazon is the way to go. Even if you are doing book signings, festivals or going door-to-door (which I don't recommend, by the way), people are still going to ask if they can find you on Amazon.

Amazon is a store, so they earn a tidy profit on sales made on their site. Make sure you take that into consideration when pricing your book. You can expect anywhere from 33-50% depending on how you set up your account.

If you are using CreateSpace, which is the Amazon print-on-demand option, you need to factor the print cost in, above and beyond the percentage they charge for selling. Print cost is based on the size of your book.

Setting up on Amazon is not hard. If you are using a distributor like IngramSpark, they do it for you. If you have done a print run, you can sell on Amazon Marketplace. Once you set up the account and name your price, when a book sells, Amazon will send you an email where to ship the book. You mail it out and confirm to Amazon and the purchaser when you mail it. You will receive a direct deposit from Amazon for the royalty as well as a flat fee for shipping.

eBooks

There is much speculation about whether print books are going the way of the dinosaurs, to be replaced with eReaders. I don't see it happening anytime in the near future. Sales for print is still keeping pace, and eBooks sales are normalizing, according to Nielson Bookscan, a media research company that tracks sales of titles.

Having your book available in both print and digital formats helps you hit a larger audience. But don't fool yourself—the formatting is different! Especially if you are working with pictures, tables or graphs. The spacing you use in print doesn't lend itself well with eBooks. Where blank pages may be appropriate in a print book to break up sections or chapters, in an eBook, a blank page looks like an error.

There are multiple formats such as mobi, ePub, pdf, pdb, txt and lrf required to allow your book to be read on different eReaders.

Smashwords is an eBook distributor that sells to just about any format other than Kindle. You only have to upload your manuscript once, and their "meat grinder" will put it in the various formats required for Apple, Kobo, Nook, etc. Getting through the meat grinder is a painful process, but Smashwords provides step-by-step instructions to help. The best part is the final product is a good one. They are a distributor, so you will pay a fee when an eBook sells, but it has only cost you time; that is, after you pay for editing and a cover, which you need for your print book anyway.

Amazon has the Kindle, so by setting up a KDP (Kindle Direct Publishing) account, you can answer a few questions and upload a Microsoft Word document. KDP will reproduce whatever you give it, so if your formatting is wrong, it won't look good on the Kindle, and you may lose readers. I haven't found an option (for free) where they proof for you. They offer a formatting service you can pay for separately.

IngramSpark will allow you to upload an eBook for distribution, but you have to already have it in ePub format, which means paying someone to do it or purchasing the software. For a fee, they will transform your book into ePub for you. They charge by the pdf page. It adds up quickly. If you don't use their service, they won't allow you to download your epub to proof before you put it out for sale to the public.

For your eBook, it's easy to change the price of your book. Before your second book comes out, you may want to drop the price of your first book to 99 cents or free. People will often take a chance for a low price, your fascinating writing will hook them and hopefully they will buy your next book.

Something worth mentioning is the idea of adjusting your pricing on eBooks for the "Long Tail." You may decide to price your book at 99 cents all the time and go for volume of sales, rather than making more money per sale with fewer sales. The good news is you can experiment and see what happens. Indie publishers may also be willing to do this; you need to discuss with your publisher.

Face-to-Face

No matter where you decide to sell your books, you should count on putting in some face-to-face time. Go to book festivals, do book signings and give talks at local libraries or schools.

If you are writing your book to support another business venture, you are probably already giving talks. Selling your book in the back of the room after your presentation is a must. There is something about the published word that lends credibility to your business.

Even a traditional publisher will expect you to be selling your book at signings and through social media. Don't shy away from connecting with your readers. Embrace it. That is how they get to know you and keep coming back for more.

If you are with an indie press or self-publishing, the face-to-face sales are the best. You cut out the distributor, therefore pocketing more of the profits. I recommend setting up a way to take credit cards through something like Square or PayPal. There are other companies. Shop around for one that works with your bank and look for the best price for the hardware, the lowest interest rate, and no monthly fee. It's best if people pay with cash, but you don't want to lose a sale because someone didn't have enough cash on them to make the purchase. Nowadays, many people make purchases with credit or debit cards. Make sure you get the hardware with a chip reader.

Pull out your notebook.

How important is it to you to get in a bookstore?

Research your best option for credit card processing.

Visit local book festivals and other signing opportunities in your area to see how others set up their tables.

Brainstorm new ideas for selling your books.

Chapter 11: Self-Publishing Route

When I first started out, I did my research and discovered when an author goes with a traditional publisher, he or she is lucky to see 5-8% in royalties.

To me, that was maddening.

I've always been a firm believer if you're going to do the work, you should get the money.

Now, in all honesty, the longer I've been publishing other authors, the more I understand the price chart. As I hope this book is demonstrating, there's a lot more to publishing than writing the book. There's a whole business behind it, requiring experts…which takes money.

Let's go back to why you are writing.

If you're writing to get famous, chances are it isn't going to happen through self-publishing. Not to say it can't happen. You may be the one who gets discovered. If so, awesome! Enjoy your fame.

I feel self-publishing (and some indie publishing) is best for people that just love to write, write as an expert to go along with their day-job, or simply want to pass something along to their loved ones.

I support self-publishing whole-heartedly, as long as the author takes it seriously and goes through the steps we've talked about in this book. Anyone can post on Amazon and call themselves an author, but sloppy publishing gives authors a bad name.

To really call yourself a published author, you need to treat this as a business. Invest in an editor and a cover artist. Learn how to format a book correctly.

So, I will go on under the assumption you want to self-publish in a professional manner.

Let's discuss some things that, if not done correctly, make a book look self-published.

> Font and size

> Headings, chapter spacing

> Margins

- Trim Size

- ISBN

- Covers

- Copyright page

Take the time to learn how to use the settings on the word processor you are using. Take advantage of the formatting tools covering mirror margins, page numbers, the custom margins, etc. The time you take up front will save you many headaches later on.

Font and size

The font is the typeface used for lettering. Most books use a font from the serif (more classic and traditional) or the sans-serif (more modern and contemporary) family for the interior. Because of the clean lines favored by sans-serif, they tend to display better on smaller screens. The font on the cover can vary widely depending on the genre of the book; different fonts can change the feel of a cover drastically.

Times New Roman is the default on many computer programs, so many self-published books tend to be published using it. There's nothing wrong with Times New Roman, and it does fall within the serif font family.

If you use a font outside the norm, the average reader probably won't notice the difference. It's one of those things people can detect when there's something wrong, but not quite put their finger on it. If you go too extreme, it's noticeable. Can you imagine reading a book written in all script?

To set your book apart, you might want to try your words in different fonts and see how they feel to you. Arial, Garamond and Palatino are just a few. You can do a quick internet search to find the latest trends.

Size goes hand-in-hand with what font you chose. Twelve-point in one is not necessarily the same size in another.

This sentence is written in 12-point Arial.

This sentence is written in 12-point Garamond.

This sentence is written in 11-point Times New Roman.

Compact fonts like Times New Roman do better in 11 or 12 points. Wider fonts like Palatino can get away with 10 or 11 points.

Novels for young adult and older are typically in the range of 11 to 12 points, depending on the font you choose. Early chapter readers have more traditional fonts but at a slightly larger font such as 14. Children's books usually have larger fonts and can sometimes get away with more playful fonts like Comic Sans. Large print books for people with failing eyesight are at least 14-18 points.

Some eReaders allow the reader to change the font and size to one most comfortable for them.

Pull out your notebook.

What font works best for your genre?

Select one page of your manuscript. Print it in various fonts, then review them side-by-side to decide what feels best.

Headings, Chapter Spacing

Chapter headings should never be smaller than the body text; the range of 14 to 16 points is comfortable. Using a different font and style (italic, bold, etc.) is common.

The title heading should not start at the top of a page. There should be a distinction to help the reader easily pick up on the change in pacing. For a novel, about one-third of the way down the page is common. Some early chapter books start at the halfway mark.

Should you use a title for your chapter? That's up to you. Often it depends on the type of story. For non-fiction, chapter titles are helpful when looking something up. For thriller fiction, a simple number is probably sufficient. For fantasy or science fiction, something more creative might stir a sense of adventure.

Pull out your notebook.

What font will you use for your chapter headings?

How far down the page will you start?

Margins

Exterior margins should be at least one-half inch to three-quarters of an inch. The interior margin, where the gutter is, should be an additional quarter inch larger than where you set the exterior margins, allowing extra room for the binding.

A nice touch is to make your bottom margin just slightly larger than the top and outside by a tenth of an inch. So, if your top and outside are .75, your bottom would be .85 and your interior would be 1 inch.

Most novels are aligned either blocked or justified, meaning the words are straight on the right side as well as the left. Children's picture books and non-fiction may vary.

For fiction, use a leading paragraph indent of .3 to .5 inches. Don't include an extra space between paragraphs.

For non-fiction you can choose to indent or not. If you don't indent, you must have extra space between the paragraphs to separate your thoughts. Do not use both an indent and an extra line between paragraphs. Choose one or the other.

Trim Size

There are a few things you need to decide before hiring a cover artist. What will the height and width of the book be (otherwise known as the trim size)? Go through the books on your shelf or check out the local bookstore. Some sizes lend themselves to certain genres. A trim size of 8"x8" is common for a children's picture book, but you wouldn't find an adult science fiction with that shape. Romance can be found smaller, 4.25"x7" ("pocketbook"). A standard trade paperback is 5"x8" or thereabouts. Non-fiction is very common in 6"x9", also a very common size for hardbacks. You can search on the internet for current industry standards.

Trim size also affects number of pages and cost of printing. The larger the pages, the fewer pages are needed, which drives the price of printing down. But, if you print on an off-size, like a novel on 8.5" x 11", it won't look right to the reader, and chances are, won't be purchased.

There are few printers that can print a large size, say 13" x 13", and it will be very expensive.

Different printers may have different standards, but they will be close to industry standards. If you want any chance to distribute to bookstores, you need to use one of the industry standard trims: 5"x8"; 5.25"x8"; 5.5"x8.5"; and 6"x9" are most common.

Pull out your notebook.

What is a common trim size for your genre?

Do you want to do hardback as well as paperback?

Is there a trim difference?

ISBN

An International Standard Book Number, or ISBN, is required for every book format, including eBook. Look on the back copy of any book you own. The ISBN is typically part of the barcode and can also be found on the copyright page.

This unique number is used internationally to identify a particular title in a specific trim size. If you print a hardback and a paperback, that's two numbers. If you print two paperbacks but in a different size, say 5x7 and 6x9, you need two different numbers.

If you produce an eBook, you can use one ISBN even if you are doing ePub, mobi, or pdf.

You can purchase ISBNs in the United States through Bowker at myidentifiers.com. You can purchase one at a time for $125 (as of this printing) or you may purchase them in bulk.

The first part of the number identifies the publisher. If you go with a publisher, they will provide the ISBN. You will only need to purchase one if you are self-publishing.

Covers

Your book cover is the "face" of your story. Hiring a professional cover designer is worth the money. Your cover needs to capture the attention of buyers so they will pick it up and read the back cover. The cover should not focus on one scene in the book (a mistake many authors make), but instead should give the overall feel of the story. Looking at the cover, the reader should instantly be able to tell the genre.

To get some inspiration, spend time at your local bookstore studying the shelves. Does the cover have a mysterious quality to it? If so, you won't be expecting nonfiction.

This sounds counter-intuitive, but you don't want your cover to be so unique it doesn't fit in with what's selling. Book designers study the trends and understand color and how they trigger certain emotions. Utilize their expertise to get readers to open the book and discover your great story.

If the front cover is catchy enough to get the reader to pick it up, they will flip it over to the back to get a taste of the story. The description on the back must capture the attention without giving away the ending. This is almost as hard to write as the actual story. I suggest writing multiple variations of this blurb and then sharing them with people you trust to give you an honest opinion. You will also use this synopsis on your website, in your metadata files used by booksellers and libraries, and in your marketing, so write carefully. Don't blow past this step.

Some books have reviews on the back cover. If you are going with an indie press or self-publishing, you'll have to get these yourself. Before I buy a book, I read the reviews but often don't recognize the name of the reviewer anyway. I would venture that's how most people are. Think about your reader-base. For a mystery, ask another mystery writer to review your book and write a blurb.

Perhaps you know other published authors. It's a good deal for them to write a blurb. It helps you and gets their name out to a wider audience. Make sure you always include the title of the reviewer, i.e. Joe Smith, Librarian at Bruton High School; or Dawn Brotherton, Author of Margie Makes a Difference. It explains to the reader why their opinion should matter, which is more important than their name (unless they are famous).

The cover designer needs to know the trim size, so she can work the layout in the correct shape.

Next, what do you want for a feel? Photos or drawings? Words only? What gives the right first impression for your story? What is trending?

In some cases, this might be a multistep process. For my third-fourth grade books, I had an illustrator draw the characters for my cover, but then I paid a cover designer to pull it all together with the title, author name, spine and back content. InDesign is the most common computer program used now, but there are many out there that are acceptable. Make sure you know what format your printer needs before you hire your cover designer. The format needs to be right or you wasted your money. Your printer may provide a required template.

If you are going to use photographs, your designer probably has a favorite place to pick them from. iStockPhoto is one option among many. Make sure you are purchasing whatever artwork you are using so you own the rights. You can't just pull something from the internet, even if it is labeled as free or common use. Again, I'm not a lawyer, but common use often limits the user to things that are not revenue generating. What is okay to use for a school paper is not necessarily allowed to be used on the cover for a book you are selling.

If you want original artwork, there are many inexpensive places to search: college students, art fairs, the internet. I don't recommend using the high school neighbor, even if he is good for his age. You need someone reliable, relatable, and old enough to enter into a contract. Because, yes, you need the artist to sign a contract to state he is doing "work for hire," so you own the copyright, not the artist. Or you may decide to give him a share of royalties for life. Talk to a lawyer.

You have to have a good working relationship with your artist—this goes for cover art as well as any illustrations you might need. The artist has to understand what you are looking for and be able to tweak the things you need to change. My high school daughter is a good artist for her age. She helps me by sketching the scenes I want, then I pass them to a paid artist to make them come to life. (I do supplement her allowance a bit for the assist.)

Your artist must also be able to meet the timelines you agree upon. If they don't meet the timeline, then what? The consequences need to be in the contract.

How much should you pay for a cover designer? There are so many "it depends" in this question it's hard to assign a number to it. If you pick graphics that cost money, it will drive your price up. If you are trying to create something complicated such as a collage, it may take more. My suggestion is to get price quotes from a number of individuals. Make sure you are comparing apples to apples by giving them the same exact specification. Review their previous work and talk to some of their clients if possible. I have found a cover designer who will lay out what I give her for less than $100.

Pull out your notebook.

Take a trip to the bookstore. Take photos of the covers you like most.

Do a search on an online bookstore. Which covers catch your eye? Your cover has to be noteworthy in a thumbnail view.

Be prepared to pass these preferences on to your cover designer so they know where to start.

Do you have a specific idea already in mind? If so, sketch it out. It doesn't have to be good. It needs to give the designer an idea.

Copyright Page

The copyright page is a necessity to capture all the key information about your book, including where a reader can get more copies. The exact order doesn't matter, but there is a semi-standard order most books follow. Check out some examples at a bookstore. You can center on the page or left-justify. The copyright is on the verso, or left-side, of the book, typically on the reverse side of the title page.

These are the significant ingredients you should include at least:

Copyright YEAR Author Name

> ie Copyright 2017 Dawn Brotherton
> If you publish multiple editions in different years, list all the years.

All rights reserved.

> Or you can use the longer version that goes something like, "All rights reserved. No part of this book may be reproduced in any form or by any electronic or mechanical means, without permission in writing from the author."

List ISBNs for all your versions

> ISBN 978-1-xxxxxx-xx-x (Hardback)
> ISBN 978-1-xxxxxx-xx-x (Paperback)
> ISBN 978-1-xxxxxx-xx-x (eBook)

Published by Blue Dragon Publishing, LLC. (if you are self-publishing, you can put your name here or don't include the "published by" line. CreateSpace is not a publisher.)

Contact information; don't use anything personal.

PO Box 247
Lightfoot, VA 23090 USA
www.blue-dragon-publishing.com
(or your author website)

Library of Congress Control Number: 2018xxxxxx

You need to file with Library of Congress to get a number or a Preassigned Control Number. The rules are very strict for self-publishers.

You may want a disclaimer similar to: "Some characters and events in this book are fictitious. Any similarity to real persons, living or dead, is coincidental and not intended by the author."

Illustrations   and   cover   by
_____

You may want to include the editor's name.

Printed in the U.S.A. (if that is the case)

Pull out your notebook.

Draft your copyright page.

Copyright (www.copyright.gov)

Copyright is a form of protection grounded in the Constitution to cover published and unpublished works. Your original work is protected under the copyright law as soon as it is created in a tangible form (ie, on paper or in the computer).

Copyrighting protects original works of authorship such as poetry, novels, movies, and songs. It does not protect facts and ideas, although it may protect the way these things are expressed.

There are many stories following the line of a princess trapped who gets saved by the prince. The idea is not copyrighted; but the creation of the actual storyline in writing is protected.

It's one thing to know something is copyrighted; it's another to have to prove it. By filing with the copyright office at www.copyright.gov, you can save yourself time, energy and money in the long run if your words are ever contested by another. If you find your book published under someone else's name, and you hold the copyright, you can take them to court. The copyright registration is considered prima facie evidence in a court of law, meaning it is accepted as true unless proven otherwise.

Copyright violation is not one of those laws you report to your local law enforcement for action. To get justice, you have to get a lawyer and go to court. It's best to have everything as clear cut as possible.

You can file for copyright on your own by going to www.copyright.gov and following the directions. There is a filing fee, and you must follow up by mailing them two copies of your "best" copy. This means, if you are printing eBook, paperback, and hardback, you should send them two copies of the hardback.

If, after filing and mailing in your books, you find an error, you can make the change and it will not affect your copyright. If you do a significant revision, you should refile using a new ISBN.

Pull out your notebook.

Bookmark the copyright website.

Review the information you will need to fill
out the copyright application.

Chapter 12: Printers

When you have your interior and cover mostly completed, it's time to send out for multiple printing quotes. You can always adjust slightly after you complete your final editing.

Even if you haven't decided on the number you want printed, pick an amount and trim size and stick to it for all the quotes so you are comparing apples to apples. Make sure to factor in shipping costs. They add up quickly.

Traditional Print Run

If you have money to invest, a traditional printing will typically give you the best price per book. A small print run can be any number of books from 50 to 1,000 depending on what you're going to use them for. The best thing about self-publishing is you can make the decision that works best for you.

I recommend you look at local printers first, which will save you shipping charges. You should always get at least three printing quotes for each book. Don't assume the best price from a printer on one book will be the best for another one. Size, page count, and format make a big difference printer-to-printer.

It's also important to have a good relationship with whomever you pick. Some printers will print whatever you provide them, where others will give you pointers and be more helpful in the process. Make sure to ask about all the fees upfront. Some will charge for every change. You will be better off paying a little more and not paying change fees, especially when you are first starting out.

Ask for their break-points, meaning at what number of books do you start receiving a price break per book. Many times it will be at 100, 200, 500, etc. Not all printers offer break-points, and even if they do, the points may be different.

You can always start with a print run and then shift over to print-on-demand when your initial sales die down (or vice versa).

Print-on-Demand

Print on demand (POD) is a good option if you don't have the money or garage space to invest in a traditional print run. The idea is when an order is placed through POD, one book will be printed and mailed to the buyer. This is a great option, but each book price will be much higher, meaning you will make less per sale.

As the author or publisher, you will be able to purchase POD books to keep on hand for book signings or review copies. POD companies don't usually offer a break-point, but your purchase is only for printing and shipping, and will not include the distribution fee.

There are two POD companies that come to mind, although there are more available. CreateSpace is the Amazon POD version, and Lightning Source is the POD for Ingram. There are plusses and minuses of each.

CreateSpace is free to setup a title, and they will even offer a free ISBN. The downside is bookstores and libraries typically will not purchase through CreateSpace because CreateSpace will not take returns. And if you use a CreateSpace ISBN, they will be identified as your publisher. You may lose a little on credibility, but it's a great way to start. And depending on why you are publishing, it may not matter to you.

If you use IngramSpark, they are a larger distributor, and you can set it up to allow for returns. Keep in mind the price will be passed on to the author if there is a return, but it does keep your options open for brick and mortar sales. As of the printing of this book, IngramSpark is considering upgrading their services to include return warehousing. If a bookstore returns a book, instead of mailing back to you as the author, IngramSpark will keep it on their shelf and mail it out next time an order comes in, rather than printing a new one. Watch for those potential changes.

A plus to POD is if you catch an error in your book, you can fix it and upload a new version very quickly. IngramSpark does charge a fee for setup and for every new version of interior or cover. CreateSpace does not charge for setup or uploading new versions.

POD companies make their money on distribution. Even though I say CreateSpace is free to setup, they will still take a percentage off every sale. Same with

IngramSpark. They charge a setup fee, printing and a percentage on each sale.

Not all formats can be done POD. For example, neither Lightning Source nor CreateSpace will do coil binding. CreateSpace doesn't do hardback.

There are other POD companies, so feel free to explore. Remember to ask about distribution and change fees.

Paper Quality

Another thing you'll have to research before asking a printer for quotes is what weight of paper you want (measured in pounds using the # symbol) and what color. White is the most common, with natural, cream, or off-white (depending on the printer) as an option. You have a choice of coated or uncoated, smooth or vellum paper.

If you are self-publishing, you can do whatever you want. There are some guidelines. For example, you don't typically print children's picture books on cream paper. To make the colors pop, white paper is standard, and a heavier paper like 70# or 80# keep the colors from showing through.

For a novel, 50# white is common. If you are writing a memoir or devotional, white or a cream color are both seen. Black and white photos in a novel show up well on 60# white or cream. If you'll have a lot of photos, you may want to go to at least 70#.

As long as you understand the basics, don't hesitate to ask the printer for their recommendation. Some printers have slightly different numbers or colors, but the concept is the same—the higher the number, the heavier or thicker the paper. There is also a slight cost difference, but don't let that deter you from making the right choice. If your final product looks cheap, it won't be appreciated.

Pull out your notebook.

How much money do you have to invest on printing?

How many do you think you can sell in the first run?

Do you have an event coming up that will make it financially advisable to do a print run?

Create a spreadsheet to collect print quotes. Make sure to give all the printers

the same information to quote from, even
if you decide to change it later.

- o Trim size

- o Paper color and weight

- o Number of pages

  Interior color vs B&W

- o Cover 4-CS (typical)

- o Cover: paperback, case laminate, or
  cloth, with or without dustcover

- o Binding: perfect (most trade books
  are perfect bound), hardback, coil,
  saddle stitch (or staple bound)

- o Shipping cost

Chapter 13: Warehouse/Fulfillment vs Distributor

If you don't go the POD route, you now have a print run of books. Depending on your goal, you may need warehousing and distribution.

A distributor is a company that has established relationships with bookstores and libraries. If they decide to carry your book (for a fee), it's their job to get your title in front of the buyers for those bigger establishments. It's not a guarantee they will actually sell anything. But as we discussed, brick-n-mortar don't have to be your goal, so this may not be a factor for you. Libraries will typically take your book if you donate it, but often won't purchase directly from an author. Your situation may be different if you have a good relationship with the librarian.

If you have a distributor, you need a warehousing company. Typically, distributors won't allow an author to act as their own warehouse.

Distributors are paid to act on behalf of the books they agree to represent in order to get them in front of bookstores and libraries. Once an order is placed, it is sent to the warehouse who acts as a fulfillment agent and sends the books to the store. They also process any returns from the store. Warehouses typically charge for storage and every time they touch a book—either to ship out or accept a return. Those costs come out of your profit.

A self-published author could probably have a warehouse and fulfillment agency if they are acting as their own sales representative, but I haven't found a distributor yet who will work without printed books stored in a warehouse to fulfill the orders they work to get. That's not to say there isn't one out there somewhere. I personally have found storing books in my garage and acting as my own fulfillment agent has made me more money than I would have paid to another company. Of course, you need to ensure your storage area is sufficiently bug-free and not too damp.

For some of the bigger distributors, Ingram and Baker & Taylor (B&T) come to mind, but it isn't a matter of simply hiring them. For B&T, they use Bookmasters as their POD company, and Bookmasters has a long application process in which the author must show past sales receipts before they will consider you as a client.

IngramSpark is the distributor for Ingram, using Lightning Source as the printer. I find them to be more user-friendly. They are continuing to evolve with the growing need of self-publishers, so check out their website for their latest services. They may add warehousing in the near future.

If you work as your own warehousing and fulfillment, you will need to be able to mail out books ordered through Amazon within 48 hours to meet their service criteria. When you go on vacation, you need to take a few books and envelopes with you in order to respond. Or have a neighbor who is willing to take on this responsibility for you.

When you ship out books, use media mail within the United States. It is the most cost effective. The buyer pays for shipping, so you should not lose money with this arrangement.

I suggest purchasing padded envelopes in bulk to save money and have them on hand.

Pull out your notebook.

Do you have the storage space for your books?

Are you willing to respond within 48 hours when a book sells?

If you want to find warehousing and fulfillment, locate at least three and receive quotes from them. Remember to use the same criteria for each requested quote.

- How much does it cost to store per month?

- Is it by book? By shelf space? By square foot?

- Is there a minimum amount required?

- How do they handle returns?

- How and when are you charged?

- Do they have an online management system where you can track the inventory?

Chapter 14: Indie Publishing Route

It's good to know the many things that go into publishing before you meet with an indie publisher so you know the questions to ask. I suggest you don't skip over the self-publishing section of this book.

If you have a publisher, the ISBN will be assigned to their company, distinguishing you from a self-published author and putting your title under their publishing umbrella. The number itself will be unique to your title.

What tasks are different between self-publishing and the indie publishing route? It depends on the publisher. Some act very much like a traditional publisher but on a smaller scale.

Author Input

With a smaller independent press, the author often works in conjunction with the publisher to create a professional product.

You need to determine what is important to you and what you are willing to let the publisher decide for you.

Will you have input into the print size, cover design and title? Does the publisher file the copyright in your name for you? Who owns the rights to publish your work? Sometimes the publisher owns the rights for a certain time period (or for life, if you aren't careful). What are your obligations to the press? How much of the costs, if any, are you required to pay? What percentage of royalties will you receive and at what point will you start collecting? Do they have foreign agents to handle overseas sales and printing? What about audio books?

If the indie publisher is set up like a traditional publisher, they will do the editing, cover design, format, and layout for no fee. Also, like a traditional, the author's royalty rate will be very small (between 10-20%). Typically, their marketing will be very minor, and distribution will not be like you would get with a large traditional, but it's worth asking about.

A hybrid-independent publisher is closer to the self-publishing end. More than likely, they will charge fees upfront for services they provide, but your royalties should be much higher. It isn't unusual to pay for editing, design work, and printing. The benefit of a hybrid publisher is you have much more creative control in the process, and when the book is complete, you own the finish product and make the decision about what's to be done with it.

Unlike a traditional press, with a hybrid publisher, the author should retain the majority of the rights and the money. The publisher will have already collected their due, therefore, the small royalty payment they receive for ongoing sales is the cost of keeping their limited sales distribution networks open and working as a go-between with the printer for you. A hybrid publisher may offer some marketing or provide additional marketing services for a fee.

Be careful you don't cross from hybrid-indie publishing into vanity press. It's good to keep your options open and be able to make decisions, but you want a partner in your publishing career, not a company to take your money and run. A proper hybrid publisher should be relieving some of the burdens you don't want to deal with, so you can focus more on writing. You should have a better product than you started with and learn something in the process. A vanity press will simply take your money and print your book. You could probably go to a copy store and run copies cheaper.

If you are dedicated to marketing and selling your books—like all publishers will require—you will most likely make more money per sale using the self-publishing method. The second highest revenue producer would be from hybrid-indie publishing.

Printing with an Indie

Some Indie Publishers will give you the choice of a print run versus POD, or a mixture of both. If you have the money to invest and the market to sell to, a print run of a few hundred books is a good way to go—assuming the publisher has a warehousing option or will allow you to warehouse your own books. The books can still be sold on Amazon through Seller Central. When a book is sold on Amazon (who still takes their percentage), the publisher is notified. They would in turn either mail the book out themselves if they are the warehousing agent or contact you to ship the book. Whoever is shipping the book should be reimbursed the shipping and handling fee Amazon charges customers.

Some indie publishers will require you to purchase a large number of books as a condition of your contract. Look closely at why they are requiring you to purchase books. If it is because they have a large distributor that requires books on hand, it might be a fair deal. If they don't have such an arrangement, it may be another way to get money from the author.

If you elect to do a print run, you can always switch to POD after your supply is depleted to keep your book alive forever. Ensure your publisher has the accounts available to do this.

Some independent publishers offer only POD which limits how much money the author can make but simplifies the process for the publishers by making it a one-size-fits-all option. Ask who the printer is. You don't want a publisher to set you up only on Amazon's CreateSpace, because you can do that yourself, and there is no added benefit of a distributor attached to it.

Make sure you shop around for the publisher that will do the most for the money you are paying. Go back and review the POD pluses and minus listed in Chapter 12.

Pull out your notebook.

Do a search online for indie-publishers to approach.

Create a spreadsheet to compare their answers.

Create a list of questions to ask potential independent publishers.

- Who is their distributor?

- Who does warehousing? Who pays for it?

- What marketing do they do?

- What costs are required upfront from the author?

- What percentage of royalties and how are they calculated?

- At what point does the author start collecting royalties? How often are they paid out (i.e., monthly, quarterly, yearly)?

- Is the Author required to purchase books?

- Who files the copyright?

- Does the publisher file with Library of Congress?

- Who holds the rights to sell your book and for how long?

- Will you have input into design?

- Add any other question you may have.

Final Thoughts

As you can see, you have many options to go from a writer to published author. The road is endless and has many side routes to explore. Remember it is a journey, and one to be enjoyed. Find the route that suits you the best for your time and situation.

Many authors have dabbled in various types of publishing over their career. Even some famous ones started with the traditional route and have now discovered the goodness and profitability of going self-published.

Remember, your manuscript is your baby. It deserves to be nurtured and treated right. You wouldn't entrust your baby to just anyone without doing your homework.

Good luck!

Recommended References:

Books

The Chicago Manual of Style

Associated Press Stylebook

On Writing by Stephen King

The Writer's Little Helper by James V Smith, Jr

Self-Publisher's Legal Handbook by Helen Sedwick

Websites

https://bubblecow.com

Writers' Beware: http://www.sfwa.org/other-resources/for-authors/writer-beware/

Writers Digest.com

HughHowey Blog

IndieBound.org

ElectricLiterature.com

Meetup.com (to find critique groups)

About the Author

Dawn Brotherton is an award-winning author and featured speaker at writing and publishing seminars. She completed her first novel, *The Obsession*, in 2010. When she realized the difficulty attracting the attention of traditional publishing houses and how much money they received from her efforts, she decided to go it alone.

As a colonel in the Air Force, Dawn was no stranger to hard work. She set up Blue Dragon Publishing, LLC and started slowly taking on other authors. She retired from the military in October 2016 and truly ramped up her business, publishing ten new books and taking six new authors under her wing within the first two years. Dawn's objective from the beginning has been to mentor people through the publishing process, helping them reach their goals. She has expanded her company to include the Author Academy, student outreach, and community service.

Blue Dragon Publishing is focused on helping a writer's dream become a reality.

Books by Dawn Brotherton

Jackie Austin Mysteries
The Obsession
Wind the Clock

Lady Tigers Series
Trish's Team (book 1)
Margie Makes a Difference (book 2)
Nicole's New Friend (book 3)
Avery Appreciates True Friendship (book 4, written by Paige Brotherton)
Tammy Tries Baseball (book 5)

Softball Scoresheet

Worth the Wait (written as Misty Austin)